Familiar Tense

SUSAN TERRIS

POETRY BOOKS BY SUSAN TERRIS

Familiar Tense, 2019

Ghost of Yesterday: New & Selected Poems, 2013

The Homelessness of Self, 2011

Contrariwise, 2009

Natural Defenses, 2004

Fire Is Favorable to the Dreamer, 2003

Curved Space, 1998

CHAPBOOKS AND ARTIST'S BOOKS

Take Two: Film Studies, 2017

Dreamcrashers, 2016

Memos, 2015

All Generalizations Are Generalizations, 2013

Tale of the Doll & the Bootless Child, 2011

Bar None, 2010

The Wonder Bread Years, 2009

Chapbook on the Marketing of the Chapbook, 2009

Double-Edged, 2009

Buzzards of Time, 2008

Marriage License, 2007

Sonya, The Doll-Wife, 2007

Block Party, 2007

Poetic License, 2004

Susan Terris: Greatest Hits, 2000

Minnesota Fishing Report, 2000

Eye of the Holocaust, 1999

Angels of Bataan, 1999

Killing in the Comfort Zone, 1995

Familiar Tense

SUSAN TERRIS

MARSH HAWK PRESS

East Rockaway, NY • 2019

ISBN-13: 978-0-9969911-4-8

Marsh Hawk Press books are published by Poetry Mailing List, Inc., a not-for-profit corporation under section 501 (c) 3 United States Internal Revenue Code.

Front Cover:
Edgar Degas, "Blanchisseuses et cheval," c. 1904. Pastel – 107 x 124 cm. Reproduced with the permission of the Musée Cantonnal des Beaux Arts, Lausanne, Switzerland.

Book design by Jeremy Thornton

Library of Congress Cataloging-in-Publication Data

Names: Terris, Susan, author.
Title: Familiar Tense / by Susan Terris.
Description: First edition. | East Rockaway, New York : Marsh Hawk Press, 2019.
Identifiers: LCCN 2018035326 | ISBN 9780996991148 (pbk.)
Classification: LCC PS3570.E6937 A6 2019 | DDC 811/.54--dc23 LC record available at https://lccn.loc.gov/2018035326

Marsh Hawk Press
P.O. Box 206, East Rockaway, N.Y. 11518-0206
www.marshhawkpress.org

For my fictional mentors
whose triumphs and failures
I carry with me into the
challenges of poetry:
Circe, Lady Macbeth,
Dorothea, Jane, Emma,
Anna K, Jo, Thomasina,
Scout, and Alice,
always Alice

Contents

II
Take Two / Film Scenes

III
The Real / The Surreal

1

The Girls / The Boys

Bad Seedling, 1929

Smocked dress, one scraggly braid but hair escaping
everywhere—dark hair, untamed Medusa-hair.

Her fingers, clenched behind her back, hold something
stolen or forbidden. Near her on the old enamel stove,

a tin tea kettle. Watch her. Carefully watch that horizon
line of her mouth. One eye is obscured by wild locks,

but the other gives a skank-eye, an eat-shit-and-die look.
Beware of what's cached in her hands but also what's

in her head. Through a glass darkly, she seeks secrets. Do
not trust the hot kettle to stay on the stove. This girl, this

little girl-woman, has ideas. She is, at six, already planning
her escape. And when she breaks out and flees,

we will—each and every one of us—be ass over teakettle.
Burnt, finished.

Alice, Always Alice

The long hair, the headband and the grinning cat.
A knight, like Quixote, who keeps sliding off
his horse. Still, she is obsessed with the real

sense that everything she attempts will fail.
All those cards and notes, and she's
again Alice throwing the deck in the air,

declaring they're a useless pack of nothing.
And yet, in the shadows of the house,
in her room, in her head, she considers

possibilities. *All risk holds the possibility for failure.*
How long is forever? she asks. Rabbit checks
his watch. *Sometimes,* he promises, *just one second.*

Becoming a Crusader

Marching. Her eyes do not blink. She is marching
but not to Georgia. There is dirt caked under her nails

and, tied with shoestrings to her eight-year-old waist,
a long snake-embossed sword.

Her overalls button at the top, are rolled at the bottom,
and have a fly front. Her eyes say: *I see you....*

They say: *No more.* They say: *I'm leaving and will
never come back.* This is a crusade, pilgrimage to save

self from the mother who looks away, from brother
whose old overalls she wears. He will never

mess with her again. It makes her no nevermind that
her sword is plastic. Do not try to stop her.

As she marches through dark into sunlight, far from
the mother, from the hands-on-her-body brother,

a she-bear will guide her. Look—the eyes, those eyes
say it all: two words, two forbidden words.

Angel Child/Bathroom Mirror

Close-up, his skin looks iced with lanugo.
Face of an Italian putto from some old fountain,

heart-shaped lips and stone-chiselled curls,
arms crossed to hide his unmuscled chest,

fringed lashes to ring his shuttered eyes. Is he
hurt or merely dreaming? Did he come

unfinished into a cold and slippery world?
Who cut the heart and left only those mocking

lips? He pulls on a striped tee. But—wait—there's
a gun here. He eyes it, palms it, slides it into

his blue/red Batman knapsack. Then he kills
the bathroom light and saunters off to school.

He's late. The lunch room is full. Because he sent
texts, they are waiting....

Cold Loaves

She takes the warm loaves out of the oven. She lights
the candles on the table. Butter is soft, jam homemade.

Wooden chairs scrape the floor. He cuts the roast into
delicate slices. No one says grace any more. They just

begin to eat. They don't look at one another. Who was
that boy they made? Who lived in their house

and ate peanut-butter-bacon sandwiches and played
baseball until his head smelled like wet dog?

Their lives now: a kind of sleepwalk. Who could go into
a school with guns? Both days and nights are long.

No neighbors or neighborhood any more. Even a trip to
the store takes nerve. No way to paper the past or paint

a future. They chew, swallow. They don't read newspapers.
No one in their house ever had a gun. They have no gun.

Then what do they have? Only the wish that they, too, had
been assaulted and bloodied and robbed of recall.

Sisters of Doom

Don't start by asking about the mud. Don't start by saying
we're an unholy trio. We are not the three monkeys who

see, hear, or speak no evil. Closer maybe to the Fates. Yes—
sisters, dirty blondes, literally and figuratively. And we are

hated, you see. Truth-tellers are always shunned. You might
swear we came from the muddy pillow fight at Glen Ellen,

but that would be a damned lie. This mud has been flung
at us, at our faces and our naked girl bodies, wet,

gritty, punishing. They, the hooded ones, stripped off
our clothes. Turned us to dirt. Soon we, the violated, will

be violating. Clo will spin the rope. Latchie will measure it.
Then Atty will cut it and them. See our unblinking eyes,

grim, filthy faces, the new-moon shadows of our budding
breasts. Take care. Beware as we gaze out at you from

the photograph you snapped—we are watching.

Boy, Dirty, Aged Twelve

He doesn't love anyone or anything. Except the kestrel
jessed on his leather-gloved left hand.

She's his, and to live, each day, she must kill.
Whatever she finds when the boy flies her — vole,

sparrow, mouse — she presents to him as trophies.
Then gripping with her dark talons, she uses her

sickle-beak to probe brain and liver, to eat them
before she dismembers and picks pink

flesh from delicate white bones. The boy is
too weak to kill, yet watch he must. Her triumph,

her skill, her pleasure make him hard, so as she
eats, he slowly does himself.

This: their ritual. They are coupled. Their love real.
And, every day as she stares into his eyes,

he whispers, *Take me. Eat my heart. Clean my bones.*

The French Girl Who Hates to Be Euridice

Mon dieu, see this heads-up girl. No Styx here
and no Charon,
nor would she have any coins for him.

She's broke and riding to the Underworld
on the Métro.
Her purse holds only a silk scarf from

Hermès, which she swiped after she stole
the leather jacket from
Bon Marché. Her t-shirt was a freebie from

an Orphée concert. Paris is expensive. A living
hell. And her cell phone is
dead, so there will be no more texts from him.

Look, he's not really her husband. And he has
groupies. Said he'd come
for her but will be late. He's always late.

Said he'd lead her back, but she may not go.
This is more like a soap opera than one by Gluck.

When he comes, she—Euri—may decide to drop
his hand. Then when
she screams, *I hate you*, he will turn his head.

The French Boy Who Must Be Faust

Lips puckered, he lounges against breasts and pubes
of satiny white marble.
This *café au lait* boy has made a bargain with the devil

and all the *jeune filles* are his for the taking. Sexy
kid, bare chest, see his ribs, boxers, three gaudy belts.

The cast on his arm is a brawling weapon, and
slung from neck to navel,
a loop of cloth long enough to hang someone.

Je m'en fiche, he whispers, ready for *Walpurgis*, eager
for orgy. Might as well take them all — caress, probe,

suck. This boy wants women. He will jab them
with his joint.
He may go to hell, but what a wicked trip it will be.

Memo to the Young Hooker

girl   you still have those eighth grade eyes
too much mascara   a bit smudged on

your forehead as if it's Ash Wednesday and
you've got Wednesday's child's air of woe

but I sense your once-upon-a-timeness
the soft spot   your parchment head cradled

was it a rabbit or rag doll you slept with
what changed   did someone beat or fondle

or were you   instead   a bright unruly kite
who snapped your twine   then lost your tail

Memo to the Girl in the Body of a Boy

not as simple as being a sissy   how to
count up the wrong two   a razor can clean or kill

if bone and bone were split   if hair didn't grow
the nightlight might burn out   if marbles

spin outside their circles   girl-brother
boy-sister   the way to hell is differently-paved

not just baseball mitts or black Allbirds   not
a wish for tutus or a bright pink bedspread but

echoes of contralto cries and of a Beethoven sonata
skin-deep is deep skin   not just one more bruise

This Was Not Her Idea

Why is the young girl with the dark, solemn face
holding in her hands the plastic mask of

a pale blond princess? Who gave her this mask,
took this picture? The girl is beautiful, clear-eyed,

wearing a new tweed coat. This photograph was
not her idea. In fact, the coat and pristine sweater

beneath may not even belong to her. Do not show
anyone this image. Tear it up. Help her stuff

that Halloween prop in the trash. Let her keep
the coat and sweater only if they are hers.

And remember her gaze. She's already becoming
a queen, one who will never need a false face.

Baby in a Plaid Blanket

We say he's my brother, but that is a lie. Fourteen,
yet I grew him inside of me. Now in Big Ugly,

it's December-cold. My jacket is thin, streaked hair
uncombed, but, since momma says fresh air is

good, I have carried him out. He's warm in
his blanket, warm against my chest. Yes, though

I know how he got in me, I will never tell. There's
black in my knuckles from digging potatoes

or from diaper changing. So what? For me, no
cross-country, no art, no 8th grade swing dance.

I walk far and farther, will leave him in the manger
at the creekside church. He does not want to

be my brother, and I do not want one more boy in
the house. "Well…goodbye," I tell him. "Have

a real good life, dude." Then his eyes snap open. Then
he grabs hold of my scuzzy hair and will not let go.

Garage Note with Rabbit

Momma—I hear the phone but can't answer.
This is not my home. I do not belong.
Everything is locked up. Each object outlined

and in place. Water seeps in from the driveway
and the mold-smell disorders the order.

Prisoner—yes, I am a prisoner here. Think of
the moth who thought fire was sunlight. All I
said was, Yes, a ride. Now the fire is a plug-in

heater. I am burned, wingless, blinded, too.
I regret yet can't regress to who I was, Mommy.

Like that dream where I swallowed a baby
rabbit who was still alive, something in me
is clawing to get out. The man with the BMW

will answer his phone. Then he'll come,
draw my outline, hang me up by the rake

and shovel. Inside me, the rabbit kit gnaws.
There is no song, no day—only dull gloom.
I am out-of-place here. Moth? Bunny?

Me? What? Why? How long....

Momma's Sugar

Big cop, big gun, small boy
Boy's sack's sugar for his momma
In his pocket, just candy and coins

Big cop with big gun hollers, *Stop*
Small boy stops, turns
Big cop yells, *Drop it, Turd*

Boy drops, sack splits, snows the street
Big cop flatfoots, hooks small jacket
Boy jerks, grabs gun

Small boy, big cop
Ain't no fun when rabbit's got the gun
Big cop howls, spins boy and gun

Fires, *Holy hell, son*
And momma's sugar's all gone

The French Girl Who Would Be Manon

Sitting cross-legged in jeans, the French girl
at the edge of a pond drops
bits of her madeleine into the mouth of

a gaping trout. She's quiet, patient, her fringe
spiking down over her eyes. But it's not girl

or fish that arrests us. It's the white scarf wound
three times around her neck
and the bracelet on her angled wrist: masks—

comedy and tragedy. Neither masks nor bold
gold hoops helped her land the part. She will

never make it. One more Manon wanna-be,
she opens her mouth as
the fish does. *Pauvre poisson*, she whispers.

No part. No lover. No art. She will need to
wind the white scarf tight, then tighter.

Boy? What Boy?

This is a story you don't want to hear. A boy found a gun
in the barn of his grandfather's ranch. He and his cousin,

playing cowboys. It was only a prank when the boy
held the gun to his head.
                    Boy, the boy—

gone. Toby, at ten, ended. Then his mother sent
my son a bright-day photograph: his friend Toby

and himself with milky moustaches and grins licking
Dairy Queen Dillies. To my son, who

dropped the photo on the kitchen floor, tragedy was
real yet not quite. But that same year he begged

us to let him see *The Godfather*. Then he wept aloud
at the severed horse head on a bed.

No . . . he cried, *Too real.* Even more real than imagining
his Toby shattered, lying on the barn floor.

Cross Country

This was a game of dares: get the girl who won't
undress or shower after a run. But when they
held her down, peeled off her shorts, her white

panties, she didn't struggle. Nor as they tore off
her t-shirt and her sports bra yet not her shoes,
ankle-tape, or socks. Mute, eyes closed, the girl lay

there as they mocked her unshaved armpits, sparse
pubic curls, the outie where an innie should have
been. They were hooting like hyenas. *Pack mentality,*

the girl told herself. Then, without moving
from the locker room floor, she began to stretch,
and then she began to run, run across a long,

swathe of meadow to a steep trail, run with
the ease of an unclothed body. She was running
pursued by a swarm of bees, a murder of crows,

a herd of asses, and she ran and kept on running
from danger, running, running, outrunning all
her pursuers, running, running, until the last

Jenny in the herd turned off the light
and closed the locker room door behind her

Anxiety Blanket Rant

Six months I've spent—this blanket draped over my head
and covering my body. Not in bed. Not by my choice.

They—those people who used to be my
parents—packed
me off to this locked place, sent me to be

shamed. All anyone can see under the blanket is
a triangle of eyes-nose-mouth as I try to remember if

I am a boy or a girl. Here, it no longer matters. Like
Emily or some Emilio, I say: *I'm Nobody. Who are you?*

Yes, there's school here and poetry, but blanketed, I
sit at a desk, not a ghost but as an anxious animal.

Why animal, you ask? This blanket, you see, has
weights sewn along its edges, like blankets

used to calm horses or dogs. But I have a plan.
Soon these people will wheel out the laundry bin with

me folded in the bottom. This Nobody will escape.
These people and those people will never again see me.

Memo to the Former Child Prodigy

by the age of nine   you knew everything   tra-la
had met two Presidents   tra-la   could explain pi

memorize Shakespeare soliloquies
or checkmate anyone blind-folded   child's play

violin   oboe   harpsichord   duplicate bridge
so what   then   was left to do

cut corners   fit in   marry someone
polish silver   slap your children   or go back

back to one   tra-la   then two and so forth
'til you learn to love all that blooms in the spring

Letter to My Daughter

Dearest, I am writing you from the banks of
the River Styx. In my hand are coins for Kharon.

But I don't have coins over each eye blinding me,
so I know Boreas is here also, purple-winged,

defeated, his hair and beard splintered with ice.
I am coming for you, at last, Kore,

with apologies for how long it's taken
to warm the globe. Now, with the death

of Winter we will be eternally reunited.
These days there are no pomegranates; and I

hope you won't mind the heat or dearth of
apples, of honey. Your summer togas are waiting.

The Lie of Acronyms

The PFH bring their FLK to the local ER because she says her stomach is feeling fluttery. The daughter's age is 12, which does still makes her... *in the treetops*....a kid. But funny-looking? Hard to describe. The ears? The almost missing chin or how she walks swaying side-to-side? We, MDs & RNs, take pity on her, treating her gently, as if she is a BQ but have to tell the raging parents that their young daughter... *rock-a-bye-baby*.... claims she has an ICP.

"No effing way she's pregnant," her volcano of a father erupts.

"Not possible," says the flustered blond-streaked mother.

Because Immaculate Conception Pregnancy only happens in the *New Testament*, we call Child Services for an OFP after the weeping child... *when the bough breaks*.... insists she's never been with a boy, but...

"...sometimes," she whispers, pointing, "I play games with him...."

PFH – Parents From Hell
FLK – Funny Looking Kid
ER – Emergency Room
MDs – Medical Doctors
RNs – Registered Nurses
BQ – Beauty Queen
ICP – Immaculate Conception Pregnancy
OFP – Order for Protection

What He Did with the Beretta

Yes, that's a real gun in his hand, a Beretta 950,
loaded, found in the drawer by his mother's bed,

cool fit for a twelve-year-old hand. A shadow
of light stripes his forehead and nose, the philtrum,

too, above soft girlish lips. In the bed, his mother's
asleep, but he needs to know *now* why his father

and step-brother left. What she did. Though his face
is choir-boy sweet, his fast-blinking eyes are

cause for alarm. As he closes one to adjust his aim,
his finger is on the trigger. He squeezes.

Percussive burst, then pinwheels of light, a shower of
mirror-shrapnel. His mother, unharmed, springs up.

He, bloody only where the slide bit his hand, lets
the gun drop. His job here is done. His mother,

awake at last, gazes and
sees him clearly, as if for the first time.

Truant: Rear View

She is eleven, alone, slumped in a stiff black chair
at a black table facing a blank gray wall.

On the table a white china cup. Her hair is shoulder
length, greasy, and her back has fragile, delicate

wings, visible because she's been stripped naked.
Even her bare butt is visible. But she will not

break, even though she knows he's coming for her.
Out the open door, she hears him knifing willow

whips over by Goose-Eye Creek. Soon he will be here.
She grabs the cup, throws and smashes it against

the gray wall. Might as well earn what she will get.
Soon he will bend her over the black chair. She will

be mute, unresponsive, will not reward him. . . .

Back Seat

We remember a quirky girl with curls but chubby,
not bully-proofed. Tear petals from a winter rose,
and strew them one by one to leave a weeping

white trail. *Died unexpectedly in her home,*
the obituary said, but the whispers say: suicide....
By pills? By razor blade? And the dog?—

Petey, the obit said. Was he barking beside
the bathroom door? Now is the season of out-of-cycle
roses and blossoming plums while sweet gum leaves

still burn. Forty-seven and alone. We knew her mother,
know her father. By hanging? Was there blood? Who
found her? Who keened? Who cleaned up? Now I turn,

and she's in the back seat of the Falcon we haven't
owned for decades, hair in her eyes, lower lip
jutted. She still can't click the seat belt closed. Stubborn

girl. Misplaced. *Go, I tell her, and take the petals.*
But she won't leave. This moment clutches—and she cries
mutely, as she shreds petals with her teeth.

Not Really Sorry

Angel face, a topknot, loose curls of dark hair.
Clean unpolished nails, false eyelashes.

Between thumb and index finger, she holds
a spliff, inhaling and inhaling, as she sees the rosin

box, smells sweat flung from a spinning head,
hears the shush of a shed tutu, the clop of pink-

ribboned shoes flung across a wooden floor.
But today, neither her head nor her warped toes

feel pain. She cannot, will not, shall never,
she reminds herself, tending the ash, inhaling yet

again, as she vows to seek out debauched putti, like
ones on old Italian fountains, only full-fleshed

and alive. Her spliff, you see, is sending the smoke
signal inked on its side and disappearing:

SORRY MOM....

The Shut Door

In chalk on the black door, someone has drawn
the world yet to come. A child—androgynous,

with a tangle of ink-dark hair—is taking that
future, using both hands to smudge it, to blur

the clouds, the ascension. Now chalk in hand,
he / she, in Oshkosh overalls and Keds, short legs

splayed, is screeching out a new vision. Here,
there are gateless fences to trap and imprison,

angry scribbles and, below, lines that might be
grass but are, instead, fire, conflagration.

We can't see the child's face, but when someone
bullies through the shut door his / her face will

be licked and crazed by the silent white flames.

II

Take Two / Film Scenes

Tears / Pablo Picasso & a Portrait of Dora Maar

                                I violate   self-satisfied
by the perfection of distortion   [abstract]   her three
breasts   round hole in a childless body   she is

butchered   crying   I love the blurred tracks from
eyes too close together   yes   a nose for an ear
a doormat   some women are   and the other Dora

thinks I left for Françoise   *women are machines*
for suffering   but the real Dora Maar   [alternate ending]
my muse   is here   the woman in tears   always

two-dimensionally mine   so each day   in one way
or another   I back her against a wall   gaze at those
bank-fish eyes   crazed body   [angle]   and hang her

then   boldly slash her with my name   *Picasso*

Model Child / Evelyn Nesbit & Her Mother

what is my real age   model
for painters [blocking] in Pittsburgh   New York   me
girl with a kissable bee-sting pout   then photographers

the stage   mother who sells me   looking for   [frame]
a rich man   to marry me or pay   Stanny pays
me   untouched   14 maybe   I love oysters   bon-bons

wind-up toys   my Red Riding Hood cape   and like
Alice   I'm girlish   famous   no books about me
yet   mother pretends to protect   looks away   I

pretend too   24th St. my Wonderland   but mother
off to Pittsburgh   leaves me   alone   with him
Stanford White   [swing]   champagne-drugged   I

wake in bed   he's naked   on my thigh   blood   no
more Wonderland   but scrambled passages   lies here
lies ahead   me and the White Rabbit   trapped   dark

blood   my name is Florence Evelyn   or Evelyn Nesbit
or Mrs. Harry Thaw   money or slut   [splice]   and mother
with pocket-money   is useless as the White Queen

By The Book / Mary Shelley & Frankenstein's Monster

married at 19   Italy   Switzerland   a wager
ghost story   [mix]   babies   dead babies   one son
her book   boats and water   her creature

a monster   wants love   her poet-husband wants
cronies   titillation   [racking]   new romance
poet drowns   still the giant   at night   keeps

coming   hideous   yet consoling   sentient
will stroke her hair   [two shot]   and will not make
babies   days he hides   fiend so cold   Satan's

companion   slight ligaments   a fellow-devil
his face and body   at night   fallen yet bearable
love   unconditional   his head in her lap
or hers in his   in darkness they go   by ship   by rail

north and north   but headaches   [night-for-night]
tremors   something is happening   she grows
strange   tumor they say   but she knows more

after sunset   Mary Shelley's daemon gets bolder
scalpels   [final cut]   sutures   her single-minded lover
slices more of her delicate brain   to add to his

Sidekicks / Sancho Panza & His Donkey Dapple

in the dark   plunge   he and I   three fathoms deep
amid moonless ruins   piteously   my friend moans
swallowed by a pit   [take]   I cry out in vain

to die would be a waste of good health
                                            and I feel
[day for night]   powerless   thinking toads   snakes
our bones gnawed white   my friend is old and rather

weak   what to do   self-comfort by approach from
the rear   not a sanctioned Catholic act   nor would it be
if I dispatch him   and with my sword   feast on

tough flesh   so how much does honor pay per hour
look   to my laments   he listens   does not
say a stupid word   if we survive   I'll crown him

poet laureate   to him   I feed my last pocketful
of crumbs   [aerial shot]   with bread all sorrows lessen
others call him Dapple   to me he is donkey or ass

sigh   ass   my addled knight   Quixote   not trapped
in a smooth-walled pit   is somewhere sliding off
Rocinante   [pull back]   while   alas   I feel my belly

shrink   as I ponder faith   loyalty   self-preservation
I   Sancho Panza   fat pudding stuffed with proverbs

Novel Pick Up / George Sand & a Montmartre Bar Patron

Because Beaudelaire calls me   stupid slut   I try to prove
him right   you see   I'm on semi-permanent leave
from fiction   and marriage   my composer   applauds

but he's grey   so by night   my sport   catch-and-release
pants and waistcoat   [cinéma vérité]   with cravat   cubebs
I prowl Montmartre's nameless cafés   [mise-en-scène]

drink sour wine   chum for willing flesh   ah   look there
belle or beau in woman's frock   rouged lips   fringed
eyes cut in my direction   [match cut]   I'll take her/him

while Chopin   who calls me muse   writes a last mazurka
I rise   meet the mark's eyes   blow him/her a smoky halo of
a kiss   angle away   behind me soft steps   then   a voice

a soft one   asks   *pardon   but are you   George Sand*

Fabular Lies / Tristan & Yseult

an uncle / king   nephew / son   Irish princess
the king's bride   nephew her escort   [skypan]   but
a forest   fox and ferns   love potion for two

no dream yet of midsummer's night   no ass head
but bride de-brided   yet wed to the king
an infernal triangle   from the king   golden plums

from her lover   his plums   sin or compulsion
the tale is complex as m'lady's braided crown
[prelap]   then poisoned lance strikes nephew / son

harp or rescue   from afar   Yseult   the tell
white sails or black   lies   Tristan's mouth foams
white   [false ending]   dies   Yseult dies

King Mark shreds all garments   but think time
travel   dense braid of fabular deceit   lovers undead
flee   forest retreat   honeysuckle and hazel

intertwine   [remake]   endure   until spring forward
     three centuries   when Mark morphs to Arthur
Tristan to Lancelot   both mad for sexy Y / Queen G

Born in Fire / Scott & Zelda Fitzgerald

named for a gypsy queen   [jump cut] my life
if ever mine played out in headlines   he stole
me   my story   ballet fever they said

demon-flame   I the singed swan   yet he no
Siegfried   [arc shot]   what we did was
never real   only seared days to reassemble

on paper   booze the besting mistress   no that's
a damned lie   she drinks from your orifices
picks your pockets   and now all the flappers

are dead   even me   the rosin box   missing
the barre too high   our passports stamped
for the wrong destination   [diffusion]   my fires

hot   then hotter   Scott has asbestos hands
          asbestos soul   flocks
of jazz-age butterflies have forgotten to flap

[looping]   he ignites   until he doesn't   can't
Zelda   un-Zelda-ed   instead of Fitz
just fizz   and both of us   rendered sparkless

It's All Greek / Maria Callas & Jackie Kennedy

I speak   *Savura*   not with whispers like yours
[sotto voce]   but my own loud   if faltering
bel canto   to say   he was never yours

a piece of paper   money promised   betrayal
comes in disguise   he said you   *Scylla*   little
coathanger of Cassini-gowns   were only vanilla

did you not know   how often we two were
in Monte Carlo or asea near Scorpios   to screw
[lap dissolve]   spoon up caviar   and screw

so delicious   your jewels were meaningless
only I knew how to polish his   and when he knew
death was near   he took the deep-red blanket to

the hospital   fondled   wrapped himself in it
my last gift   bloody-strong   our love   now he's
gone   and I the grieving widow   [out-take]

yes   I am Callas   to you   Jacqueline
I send raspberries and catcalls

Familiar Tense / Mary Cassatt & Edgar Degas

    no diaries   no other letters   only this
when Mary's Belgian griffon died   the painter
  wrote   asking friends   to find her a new dog

[clip]   she was thirty-three   autumn in Paris
and send it to her by parcel post   she desires
a young dog   a very young one that will love her

artists together   again and again   he paints her

[dailies]   yet restraint   she glazes his oils
he adds highlights to hers   careful not to nudge
with his elbow   loathe to let flesh spoil luster

the new pup in her arms   she leans forward
[pull back]   a shadow union   he feels the heat
of her breath   *like the autumn we met*   *let's*

risk   she murmurs   *don't*   he cautions
I'm just an old man who likes horses as you like dogs
Mary Cassatt strokes the dog's muzzle

its silken warmth   [mask]   *when we met*   she
says   *then*   *I began to live*   Degas leans back
in the bentwood chair   closes his eyes   *tais toi*

he says   *be still*

Special Relativity / Albert Einstein & Mileva Máric

Speed of light in a vacuum   first before marriage
specific gravity   our giveaway girlchild
two scientists   scientists measure passion too

his counted   not mine   always alpha then beta
[aperture]   I agreed   we wed   velocity   two boys
those fast moving bodies   but then curved space

mistress-cousin   it's all relative   his drawn contract

neutered   made me   de-facto   no continuity
neither speech nor sex permitted   [fisheye lens]
I took the boys   left   yet that's not what you

want   [godspot effect]   you ask for   the red spread
Elsa   plates hurled   tears   the tearing of hair
we physicists seek free-falling states   time

dilation   those elementary particles   knowledge
is never filmic   what you need is
the why of Nobel cash   [reel]   what divorce

terms promised for a prize   not-yet-won
why I never said I helped   [negative cut]   was it
all Einstein   that constant speed   or Mileva too

me   with money   bribed
again   [focus then fade]   for silence

Cross / Herbert Hoover & Clyde Tolson

it's 1975   pacing up and down   the River Styx
again   the Man checks his watch   he had expected
expected St. Peter   clouds of glory   he hadn't

believed he'd be sent here   in his pockets   coins
yet he doesn't want the Underworld
[swish pan]   who will select his double-breasted

suits   will buff his calluses and paint his toenails
who else to share FBI Fizzes   to sit near the river
tieless   talking legacy   Dillinger   the subversives

to chuckle at hints of Negro blood   [rushes]   of gay-ity
three years is a long time   but the Man crosses
commandeers a deck chair   waits

for his alter ego   bosom buddy   Tolson will
bring cash and a valise to J. Edna   [pace]   Hoover is
a mess   his   and Eleanor blue tie

though he brushes them daily   are threadbare
his underwear too   he needs
[shock cut]   bras   new thongs   a black girdle

Royal Pain / The Duke & Duchess of Windsor

once upon a time   she whispers   *there was a girl*
named Goldilocks   then he says   *who went for a walk in*
the woods   [splice]   La Caravelle   champagne   paté

I still love you   he says   *Ditto   dear*   she murmurs
but *you and I create only disaster together*   so then
he says   his entrée is woefully underdone   [filter]

long wordless silence   they *are* being watched
            crimping a small rosy kerchief   he blows
his nose   more silence   [slow-mo]   she leans in so

no one can hear   *and Goldilocks   said   this porridge*
is too cold   the Duke of Windsor squares
his shoulders   replies   *but this one   is just right*

so I shall eat it all   the Duchess   reaches for his hand
finis   she says   *we may have love*   [block]   *but there's*
nothing   my darling   worse than   outliving romance

Pact / Sally Hemings & Thomas Jefferson

he never calls me girl or you   instead   Sarah, or
    sometimes   Venus   I wear Irish linens
sleek cotton stockings [adaptation]   though I speak

what   you thought I   a slave   would speak pidgin

fourteen-year-old French   I do not read well   nor do
I sleep in the small closet above his room   ours not
quite a love match but a pact   where I lie for

him and with him   but our children are all mine
though [backdrop] sometimes when I am
on my back beneath him   he calls me Martha

you see   I am pale   comely   well-educated to be

his dead wife   my half-sister   but not tonight as I
jaybird-naked   open my legs   he is fierce
I cry out   weep   kick   bite   but he laughs

cups me softly   says   now roll back   together
we shall make one more sweet child who can
pass   [catharsis]   he says   and one day

equal to Master Jefferson in voice and in sin

I'll set your babies free   and maybe you   Sarah
Hemings   proud unknowable hell-cat
you for whom my heart   [coquette noir]   beats

Dashboard Scene / Bonnie Parker & Clyde Barrow

passenger seat   arrows   boots on the dashboard
cowboy toes and frayed heels   but women's boots
leather-laced   and it's a truck   on the left

steering wheel on the left too   long mid-western
road forks ahead   [pan]   circles   maybe a gyre
a dark steel quonset hut   black-and-white magpies

she rides shotgun   feet on the dashboard
asks   *did my mother do this at my age   did yours*
arrows are invisible   yet there   they prick her flesh

radio gone   truck speeds by   if she is smoking
we can't see or smell it   but we know   in her lap
[dolly shot]   she cradles the guns

what is down the dotted line of the road
is this Bonnie   is that Clyde driving the wrong
side   yes   [master shot]   they don't know   yes

even closer   magpies   then they croon
how someone *lies over the ocean*   croon 'til they see
a road block ahead   *stop*   she cries   *stop now*

The Bloodied Bed / Lady Macbeth & King Duncan

he is slain   and we are in the burgundy chamber
half-hidden by arras   knife   much blood   little
struggle   more a death-dance   then nothing

he seems to breathe   yet not   men come   roll
the body in brocade swags   bear it away   now
we are alone [close-up]   a table   a candle   a key

a feather too   we place the key   the feather   in
our robe's pocket   try out   the bloodied bed
then rising   lift the candle   creep into the next

room   there we watch   as golden wax scalds
our hand   drips onto stone   and men tend
the corpse   [splice]   when his body's oiled   we

no I   Lady Macbeth   bend to kiss his lips   but he
eases from the pallet   Duncan becomes an arching
shadow   palms the feather   the key   snuffs

the candle   we are chilled   here tonight   Duncan
came   and purposed to leave   and he leaves us
now   here   bloodied   and darkly alone   [cut]

Interview, December 1962 / Sylvia Plath

I keep wondering why you married him.

                               Trying to chase the darkness, Sylvia says

And then the children. . . .

                               Little lights, but more darkness, she says

And your poems? Does he critique them?

                               Ted says they are darkling thrushes

Everyone thinks you're all Scott and Zelda.

                               In the dark, says Sylvia, they are all the same

Does that make you the shrew?

                               Darkness at night, she says, and at noon

And life, your life—is that all?

                               Yes, we see through a glass darkly

Then who are you? Where are you going?

                               I came from darkness, she says, and there I will return

Eclipsed / Assia Wevill & Ted Hughes

chemistry   fuck without restraint   but between
us   omens   *she*   mad phantom   haunts
taunts   *she*   hell-bent   makes all babes pay

oven gas   now   we   in his old house
   his children   his rules   yes   you vamp
[flashback]   less fetching in pinnies   shrew who

usurps   uses *her* dishes   portents   *her* sewing
basket   even *her* chenille dressing/undressing gown
owl's cry   housekeeper   I make the porridge

wipe snot   rooster-man   pecks me to submit
I aim *her* tomato soup cake   at his head
dung beetle   easy   old slag   needy hen

half-yenta queen   wanting *her* wedding ring
[extreme long shot]   oh   mister-led-by-his cock
spirit-killer   how you say *Ass-ia*   you

who only half-admit our child   murderer
Assia says   philanderer   well   just Brenda
or Carol   and forever in my face   Sylvia

no   Ted   you in ours   but we shall punish
[fade in]   daughter and I   will mock
all who love Sylvia   the oven for us two   too

Immortal / Medea's Sons—Mermerus & Pheres

call us the lost ones   the slain   [flip]   young bones
and blood   cry out   beneath this marble tomb
don't name our mother   unless you pause

passerby   I am a mute rock but these inscriptions

name our father   mother murdered for the fleece
then his new wife-to-be   yet not us   whom Hera
swore immortal   *stop*   our mother howled

tried to shield us   but no knife
fierce   [flashback]   men of Corinth stoned us

battered   bloodied   left   death-in-life
Medea   Circe's kin   another sorceress
could not conjure us back   no mandrake

must speak   so you know who hides within me

or balm   while Jason   false father   fled
we are   Mermerus and Pheres   [wipe]   abandoned
by the Corinth Odeum   this   our immortality

no chariot race skyward   and over Styx   no ferry

She-Fiend / Beowulf & Grendel's Mother

old tale   a mother   son dead   bereft   greedy for
man-blood   she-fiend   not misshapen wolf-monster
[ellipsis]   but woman   nails and sword

to kill her   Hero of Heorot   must defy fen-spirits

moor-walkers   [flux]   past earthlight
into hell-cursed water   the Geat breeches death
in murked-mere   with writhing water-worms

as dark mad-brute woman   claws   drags with
nail-teeth   to sea-chill rockchamber   and tops
him   orgy   struggle   he-she   in cave-fire light

she-demon   death-grind   she on his chest
fire-eyes   Beowulf manned and unmanned
penetration   revenge   [fog level]   the little death

another come   his weapon weak   mantis-like
she wants his head   but he hefts her sword
beheads   her dead son Grendel too   mere-blood

Grendel's gore-head speared then   and lofted

consummation   [long take]   waters roil-red
Beowulf   defiled   but still   alive

Black Jack / Branwell Bronte & His Drinking Mug

is it my carrot top   or the pale sisters   painted
yet myself removed   turned into a sloe-eyed pillar
since I am not quite real   crave gin and poppies

Black Jack for sleep   sin-steeped   set my bed afire
for I lust   keen to peel off their gossamer collars
[blow-up]   unhook   denude   taste cherries

and Black Jack hidden down there   Anne in
a book-lined study   a heathered heath for Emily
then for Charlotte   my Charlotte   castles in Angria

I   the intruder   am ill   enslaved by the unreal
what I want   to die standing up   like my pillar
but even more   [climax]   true friend to Branwell

Bronte   I want Black Jack   mine   theirs
and that sodding poppy   sweet canker-rose of Lethe

Star-Takers / Abélard & Héloïse

for each sin   in time   [reverse angle]   asks of us
asks the we   of us   breasts   brief   heedless
night steps   on stone floors   her chamber   mine

yes   her uncle's house   Paris   servants mum
she   girl-woman   *nominatissima*: intellect
renowned   and I   he   philosopher-scholar

my tutor in theory   in medicine   in company
subtle   yet   a house can be chill
so in the dark   down pillow lolls   comforters

his hands beneath my shift   bedcreaks   cries
   then   I fell pregnant with his child
our Astrolabe star-taker   and marriage   [backlit]

too late for us   for my Héloïse a nunnery
[wipe]   for my Abélard the knife   the we
of us severed   like his   no   like my manhood

our letters cold   mind ticks   shadows   the we
now   [voice-over]   only I and I

Crosscut / Jack The Ripper & Two Hookers

tricked out in gay ruffles   feathers   mesh hose
we choose to be   girly-bait   saunter
streets alone   yet together   the London fog

slimes us   wet mackerel smell   perfume
   clicks of our worn boots on cobbles
one pair scarlet   one toad green   as he

[tilt shot]   strolls our shite-pocked lanes   cane
leather apron slung as a cape   his tall top hat
satined by dank air   gestures   we nod link

arms   lead him to a room   a bed   he laughs

high sharp sounds   but under our cloaks
knuckledusters   notched blades   cudgels
he flashes his knife   but Whitechapel rules   we

are two   faster   our blades   blood
thrust   [pull back]   mutilate   we slash
his coat vest and shirt   no more sister deaths

but on his hairless chest   chemise   bound breasts
no Jack here   but a Jill   [fade to black]

sever   cut   cleave   dump in the Thames
done   the Ripper is done   [catharsis]
she is   forever   stopped

Whatever Self / Virginia Woolf & Virginia Woolf

last night   we had a dream   [fade]   the nerve of pleasure
easily numbs   a disconnected rhapsody
but we read books and write them   have a husband

a woman lover   in the garden   already
snow drops   now   copying our recipe for cottage loaf
now re-reading Byron's *Don Juan*   and gorging on

Jane Austen   Rebecca West says men are snobs   but
though we are   jam and butter   Leonard is not

today   we shy in the shadows   today the little owl is
calling   keeps calling   to silence him
we permit Clive to visit   then Lady Colefax

[dissolve]   when Conrad died   we wrote something   what
Clarissa is important   why   here is a nervous breakdown
in miniature   yesterday we had *daube de boeuf*   then

last night   the dream   the waves   waves   we are
re-editing the death chapter   though we don't get
out of bed   but shadows thin   we have tea   look at

antiques   then   ants in our brain   painted flies
in glass cages   for there we were   in last night's dream
with rocks   [follow-shot]   walking into the Ouse

it's dark now   darker   one of the Virginias must stir
make us   a simple supper of haddock and sausage

The Real / The Surreal

Lucid Dream

Before me, dark opals of babies' eyes,
prick of gorse and manzanita. I am waking

this morning as a woman who bakes bread
and sweeps the front steps every day.

Here where arrowed hands alter to
spin counterclockwise, I am rocking a baby

who babbles me messages from the past.
Here the remains of a fine woman whose rants

tug me deep inside, and that's where I need
to go. From a candle: the spill of teardrops,

a waxen thumbprint, a wing of light that
leads me, childless again, out where

a timpani of wild grasses stir the air,
where death-tinted water leaches from clouds

and, from the heart of the madrone, a minor
key tune. A fine ruin on a wet day with

the sound of crying, the smell of a sleeping
woman and of phantom bread rising

Visit from Donald Justice

The door opens. My digital clock blinks 3:01. I sit.
I'm feverish and alone in the back bedroom.

Justice, a poet, man I've never met, wearing jeans
and a black turtleneck, stands in the doorway.

His hair is buzz-cut gray. His feet are bare.
I don't flick on the light or move from the bed.

The moon, bright through the white-latticed
window, glints his hair like snow.

An apparition, maybe, yet he seems real—a time
and space gyre. I should be alarmed to see him.

He's long dead, and I am just post-surgery, but,
as far as I know, alive. I lean forward,

Where, I ask, *are your shoes?* He starts, then stops,
is closer yet still in the doorway, moonlight

carving his face to a mask. *What?* I ask, as he begins
to retreat. *Attention,* he says with a half-smile.

Pay attention. Then, as he tilts away, he calls back,
By the door. Yes, there, by the door is the place to begin.

Still His House

The husband, brain webbed by dementia, enters
the house, walks upstairs to the bedroom with

a live mouse on his shoulder. It's grey-brown,
hunched. The woman moves closer. It's not a mouse

but an orb-weaver. The husband must have
breached a garden web on his way in. *Spider,* she

says. The husband looks in the mirror. *Spider,* he
repeats. Then, slowly, he remembers and plucks

the orb-weaver from his shoulder. In this house,
still his house, no one kills a spider. To kill one in

a house brings bad luck. The husband has bad luck
already. Doesn't need more, so cupping the ticklish

creature in his hands, he carries it down the stairs,
then outside, and frees it next to the broken web.

Old Beard

I am sending back the key

– Sylvia Plath, "Bluebeard"

Till death do us part. Did it seem romantic
then, as a girl without art.

Coming to your house, your heart. The beard
I married, though, is disappearing and has

darted, perhaps, into some rabbit lair
in search of the Alice I was and there

I can see / my x-rayed heart

which makes me fear death in life more than
death, so, to start, I return the key....

Lying Down in Darkness

Are you going to get up in darkness? he asks me.
Go to bed in darkness? Turn out the light.

The basin is full of darkness. Were your
feet in it? No one can use it when it's filled

with darkness. Who killed the light and made
darkness. I want to be home now. This is

home? I'm not going to forget this. The window
is open. The heat is on hold. Not me.

In the little white cup there, pills. My pills.
Is it time? The garbage should go out, but it's

dark, and darkness paints me black. I need
more light. There are two pairs of pajamas here.

Can't wear both but can change. Why are you
angry? What makes it dark? I keep forgetting....

Clean-Up Man

In his binoculars, the man thought he saw a circling
of eagles, but I saw turkey vultures.

Something nearby was dead. Eat or be eaten. Once in
Botswana, we watched a pride scrabbling

inside a buffalo carcass as the sated lion and his mate,
half-awake, alert for vultures or hyena, lay nearby.

This man, to his own pride known as the garbage-man
or clean-up man, scavenged left-over food from all

our plates. Now appetite and senses dulled, he eats less,
has forgotten waste, dead meat, the words for vulture,

hawk, osprey. When he scans the sky with binoculars,
the only name that remains is eagle, the eagle....

Like It Was

I want to be part of your program, he said.
There is no program.

I don't like it here. I want it like it was.
We all want it like it was.

Then where's the map?
There is no map.

But, listen, I love you.
And I love you.

Doesn't seem like it. Then why am I here?
You attacked me. You hurt me.

But I want to be on your program, he said.
There is no more program....

Acorn Caps as Metaphor

Physical death is much discussed, but few
will talk about the end of love—

not rupture or even separation, more
a stutter of lost momentum. To grasp this,

go back to the doghouse tea parties
with upturned acorn caps as cups, to that

girlish idyll when love seemed to have
no conditions. Today, this September day,

angling back, my feet dragging in tanbark,
I rock on a fiberglass sheep in a child's

playground, then pump a chainlink swing,
trying to catch the lost high of infatuation

and promise. Instead, I see my husband,
memory gone, until nothing remains but

latent bouts of anger. Here, up north,
the trees have forgotten green, too; and if I

dig down, I may strike permafrost, won't
know how *I do* became

I don't, how sweet acorn tea cups
pocketed today turned into little death caps.

Ghost Note

the one I didn't write   odd   yet written in my hand
backwards slant   disappearing ink or lemon juice

practice run   to read it light a match and char   unsung
song   the missing beat   fires you covet   silenced by

hearbeat or drum   in this eternal rain   there is sun
yet no golden pot   invisible feet of striders   is that

a dog's sharp bark or treefall   is a hart leaping over
words and woods   ghost sounds   love me

then   ghost shadows   secrets   now inversion
always   ghost note   and at then last   one slow dance

The Vanished

A woman with bird feet and a baby in her arms is
humming. A rag rug braided by great grandmother

is tacked to the ceiling. Empty bookcases hang
from there, too. Why empty? Why does the curtain

billow from the top of the window and where
have the chairs and sofas gone? Howard Hughes

and Conrad are pissing in the kitchen sink. We can
hear them, their deep chuckles, too. But how will

Howard wash his hands, and what has become
of the humming woman? Are we coming or going?

The wind must be a good one, a west wind luffing
the curtain, as we stretch across the rug on

the ceiling. Though Conrad has returned, Howard
has not. But the bird woman has reappeared,

dancing across the walls with Conrad, then dusting
shelves with one corner of her shawl. She has

dropped the swaddled baby. Gracefully, the silent
child floats up to where we lie. We reach, catch

her, hold her and drift out the window, unsure
if the baby is flesh or only a passing dream.

Slow-Quick-Slow

a vagabond   slow-quick-slow   honey vanilla
he likes to keep it simple   no pieces that don't fit

still 53   seductive   and in moon-shaped cakes
unforeseen fortunes await   but read the fine print

tastes degrade with time   think agave not honey
never choose the fine print   under his hat or belt

up close   his potted plant is a forest of papyrus
pluck it   pulp it   press it   offer a vanilla response

in print or imprints   I do not like things simple
drifter   you left your horse   quick-slow-quick

tethered at the river   so how do you hope to know
what waits for you around the next bend

Something Has to Matter

Passing wet chicory that lies in the field like sky
— Michael Ondaatje, *Coming Through Slaughter*

As pollen sluiced the air, the gypsy watched a woman
in a white dress, woman who hummed as she danced

with a white pig in a blue field. She was, he decided,
one who would count spiders in her house and not
turn a tap without making sure each was safe.

Ungrounded, she seemed at home in a vaporous sky.

Safety is in the underorb, where a gypsy must have
a sleight touch to stretch the web and snag an old tale:

this one—troubadour of the mind—cloaked himself in
cloud then, playing a game, tried to stand unseen in
a meadow while a woman waltzed with a pig.

Who, the woman asked, the invisible visible, *are you?*

Instead of an ancient lute or bow, his sack held a note-
book and pen. *Does it matter?* he shrugged.

Everything matters, she said, dismissing the pig, turning
away, white wisp moving barefoot through chicory
and a whine of bright-winged bees.

Pollen-stunned, he blinked, and she was gone.

In this meadow of the unreal, he could hear the treble
of her voice yet no footsteps, no shadow-woman.

That sly spirit—mask and blue-eyed flowers haloed
with dust—was out of reach now
under the summer sun's white-hot eye.

Banished, vanished leaving only waltz-prints in blue

and the ghost of her white song. He'd steal it if he could—
that idle, other-worldly tune: matter but no matter.

Oryx Dream

On the savannah, not Rilke's unicorn or Jarrell's
eland, but you, Oryx. In the fringed grass of

the little rains, you stalk with sheen and grace.
When you bend low to browse, I mount, ride

bareback, clutching the twisted spires of your horns
as you bolt away. But you must never climb

the stairs to my house. Never expect a place
laid out at our table. Nor should you

appear one-horned to breech the gate of
my hermit's retreat. Instead, as I grip your

smoky flanks with my legs, lead me deep,
then deeper into the wet, wild caldera of time.

Silverback Dream

Under an arc of fringed-leaf bamboo, you lounge,
as always, ringed by a troop of ardent females.

I am watching without watching, knees to
chest, angled away, the ripe fruit in my palm

uneaten. What is it you want? So well-defended,
who can say? But I want a sun-warmed clearing,

you close, so we can touch finger to finger
and act as if the others do not exist.

Feigning sleep, I—aware of your steady gaze—
dare you to court me. So, Silverback, call out,

knuckle over to my vine-laced nest. Be present,
and pretend, just this once, you want only me.

Sometimes a Horse is Not a Horse

The Marais—where we are—but in another era, before chic.
And in the weed-choked square, a crowd near a creature,
legs loping in air while his grounded body writhes.
Pressing on, we hear the orgasmic wheeze of his panic.

J'ai un cheval noir et blanc.

We scramble. He scumbles, and we cling to his back—horse
with two eyes on one side of his head, reeking of linseed oil,
his canvas flanks heaving. Noir fantasy? Rescue? Ours?
His? Blank-minded and without bit or reins, we lope on.

Le cheval a la couleur de neige et de nuit.

We flee on a mirage of a mirage escaped from the musée.
All the creatures have fled—cat, goat, dogs, a circus
pursues us, as does snow and lowering night. Cut-eyed,
the horse strains forward amid yowls, bleats, barks.

Le cheval a l'air d'un rêve et d'un sourire.

I—yes—I've left my several selves, am paired with him,
I promised, he says, *promised we'd run*. Slow smile of a dream,
my thighs gripping the myth. No bridle, yet he and I
are the we in this fierce, fatal, fast-moving frame.

Memo to the Man Who Gave Me
His Mother's Wedding Ring

by mistake   after all the times   like Emma Bovary
I'd begged for a ring   but there caught in the bottom of

the suede pouch with the heishi   gift for my birthday
that gold ring with an arc of rose-cut diamonds

a thirties kind of piece   older than you think   maybe
your mother's mother's and yet   for five months

mine   but too small for my fingers   and not mine except
as love unbanded   each stone sharp enough to cut glass

Listen, Young Lover...

I've met that woman who won't wash her hair until
it rains. Then she waits for sunshine and for
dragonflies to light on her wrist. The magic of tiny

feet tickling its surface helps her to stand statue-still
until that hair has curled. Will you be enthralled if
I tell you of her collection of mason jars where

each holds a singular display: a jar of black dice,
jar filled with monarch wings and one with bullets.
She has a jar with a key from every place she's ever

lived and another with every bandaid peeled from
her fingers. Not a maiden with a mandolin,
but she coaxes shivered whines from a handsaw,

dances to thwack of an axe, and mallets empty
pill bottles like a xylophone. When she was twelve,
a would-be taxidermist, she skinned trapped mice

to make a stiff gray cape for her sister's doll.
But now she's looking for an ape-skin and fishtail
to create a mermaid crowned with her own

silky seaweed hair. Lover, she may enchant you,
but don't propose. You won't relish what follows.
Your future may include a saw, mallets, needles and

you—an object—not in a jar but nailed upon a wall.

Full Fathom Five

Instead of a kiss, he gives me a pearl button. Neither Peter Pan
nor a Lost Boy, yet the nuance is the same: a nubbin of value /

no value, something for my sewing bin, a token to save for
a rainy day, as I, too, am being saved. Pearl of wisdom, pearl as

biography, Zipangu pearl placed on the tongue of
the dead. Full fathom five, a sea change would be needed.

Of course, the button—*button, button, who's got the button?*
I do, yet it's not a kiss or even a real pearl but stamped from

mollusk shell. So this sphere in my hand will never
couple his shadow to mine. Inert, it will rattle in the bin

of the lost, sink to the bottom, cast away and forgotten amid
bright bits of plastic and leather and bone.

Pressure Points

White stones, the masseuse tells me. *When I work, I'm
pushing smooth white stones down a long white river.*

Those white stones are everywhere—slick with
water—falling and falling. *Don't fall for me,* I once

warned my would-be lover, as we skipped flat
rocks across the surface of a stream, *because I play*

for keeps. Now, face-to-face from opposite banks,
we lob the stones of yesterday: our moons,

our dreams, our bloodless failures, while
the masseuse kneads her fingers into pressure

points along my back. As I try to quiet pain,
a rock glances off my shoulder, then one grazes

my cheek. These—flung from the far shore.
Why, I shout over milky water, *are there only stones*

of yesterday? What happened to tomorrow?
My lover is mute. When he kicks his rockpile into

the river, turns away, I cry out. *Am I hurting you?*
the masseuse asks, probing for one more white stone.

Delphic Bee Dream

The honey bee of myth, of eloquence, sense,
immortality. Neither worker nor drone, I aspire

to be queen. My colony, my predictions, my
swarm, to be open to drones and dreams, to be

unmoved by death. The prick of beauty and power:
oh, the waggle dance, the round dance, all for

my continued life. You, however, seem to be
a diploid, one who escaped the fate of

ritual murder. Despite your sex, you aspire to be
a queenly king. So we shall fight for it—sting and

sting unto death. And I shall triumph. My hive,
my honey, Honey. The future is mine.

How Careless I Was to Lose
Both My Husband and My Lover

Each night, I prop two pillows under my head, and one
        behind me, stand-in

for my lost lover. Between the pillow and my back, I tuck
        a fleshy water bottle.

Charvet ties and suits once worn by my dead spouse hang
        now under the basement stairs.

He'd be crazed by that, by toilet rolls stored in his armoire, by
        the pillowman there under my spread.

I have a safe here but can't lock it. The key won't turn, and I'll
        never feel safe again.

Near the bed, the philodendron is drooping. Rootbound,
        it sheds its heart-shaped leaves.

Love Note to an Empty Bed

Across from me, a black/white picture of
a white, sheet-tangled bed by a window shot with

sunbeams. Opposite, I am lying on a white bed
by a window where the sun streaks in

as I hear wave rumble roughing the white sand.
A blaze of light from my window is framing

the other window and that white bed.
In the picture, the bed is empty. But a couple has

been there—pillows dented, sheet pulled loose
from both sides. Now, though, I have breached

their space to see if they'll return and who they
may be, I gaze back to the unmade bed I'd

left, by tufted pampas grass and the sea, the bed
I'd slept in alone.

But still on the black/white side, in reflected light,
I wait, wondering if the couple gone from

this sex-rumpled bed can be you, my love,
with some two-dimensional woman who is not me.

Memo to the Cat Who Keeps Bringing Me Half-Dead Birds

tremor of wounded breast   twitch of wing remembering
for these gifts   Grimalkin   I do not thank you

love comes in many forms   the almost moribund I know
too well   so stop reminding me   fangs are everywhere

ding-dong-bell   my own heart pierced often by words
or by neglect   like it or not   stop   we all feel pain

What's in a Name

In the language of spiders, I am known as Silk.
In the percussion of shipyards, I am known as Bell.

The past is yellow and red and laddered....
Up and down the rungs my old lovers still roam.

In the slang of the circus, I am known as Wander.
In the screech of the henhouse, I'm known as Fox.

In my own tongue, I'm called Risk or called Dare.
If you have to ask why,

you—with my old lovers—will get kicked off those
red/yellow rungs into the blue/black void below.

Thirst / No Thirst

What is it that's lost? The map and the trail,
air strummed by the wings of bees, dance of

a wet California morning, prowl through
an apple orchard, collecting windfall.

I've forgotten how to use a cider press.
Time has escaped, left me no juice, no map.

Now I prowl on my own through a hard, dry
wasteland. No rolled pantlegs. No apples.

Just a prowl with racking thirst. No tool
but a spade to dig to China or to yesterday.

So thirsty. Wasting, until it begins to rain,
and I stand with mouth open,

arms outstretched. The rain—how consoling—
tastes of old honey and of summer dust.

Spiritual Carabiner

All the fathers are dead. Now the mothers are dead, too.
And the husbands. So, for consolation, with a rope, a d-ring,

she hangs her lyra in the garden. Under the Douglas fir, it
shivers in the wind light-sparking the winter grass.

With her body curved into its silver arc, she tries to bring
back the circus and how she, rocked by the smell of sawdust,

appeared to swim in and out through the air above. But, alas,
there was no sawdust, no circus—only the lyra, its bright

promise, its circle of infinity. Once she'd dreamed drumbeat
parades, a Ringling triumph, expected a free-running

rope of time. And the lyra? An old gift, a prompt
from her mother, her father for heights still to be scaled.

Do you talk to them? a friend asked. *Or to your husbands?*
Never, she said. But she sees their many faces, younger

ones, staring from the lyra's mirrored ring. Aware then of
being watched, hoping the carabiner won't unlatch,

she begins to grip the hoop, angle her body in and out,
ignoring winter's frost, skimming the air, morphing to

a cobbled yet savvy version of the self she once wanted
to be. No...she never talks to the dead, but they

whisper, hum, speak to her, urging her to keep faith with
those who lie in the dust and to keep on keeping on.

Dish of Mashed Peas

Some people are not destined for happiness,
   and I may be one of them.

You see, in certain parts of the world where
   I have been and now live,

at least in my dreams, happiness is only
   granted to a woman

who leaves a dish of mashed peas out in
   the moonlight overnight.

But superstition does not name what moon
   phase or if one must

eat the peas. Instructions too vague.
   Peas uneaten. Moon dark.

No happiness yet. I'd ask my nana if she
   were still here,

but she was the one who gauged oven heat
   with a bent elbow

and said happiness was to bake a cake
   until done.

Sockeye Dream

Salt water swimmer with freshwater memory,
years spent displaced but yearning,

let me follow you. I, too, remember upstream,
its pine-dusted air and scent. When you look

for that place which you, as a sleek fry, called
home—take me along. I, too, need to

thrash past fern, over current-smoothed rock,
struggle toward a pinked dream-spot.

As I travel with you, broad river to stream to
inlet to pool, your quicksilver tail will be

my beacon. And I, too, will think love
and think *home, home*—instead of only death

Acknowledgments

About Place, South: *Baby in a Plaid Blanket*

American Journal of Poetry: *Take Two: Eclipsed; Take Two: Pact*

American Literary Review: *Sockeye Dream*

Arts & Letters: *The French Girl Who Hates to be Euridice;
The French Boy Who Must Be Faust; Oryx Dream; Delphic Bee Dream*

Blue Fifth Review: *Take Two: Tears; Take Two: Immortal;
Take Two: Star-Takers*

Catamaran: *Lucid Dream*

Colorado Review: *Take Two: Sidekicks*

Connotation Press: An Online Artifact: *Memo to the Girl in the
Body of a Boy*

Cumberland River Review: *Truant: Rear View; Not Really Sorry*

Denver Quarterly: *Memo to the Former Child Prodigy*

Diode: *Take Two: Cross*

FIELD: *Lying Down in Darkness; Full Fathom Five*

Georgia Review: *Boy Dirty, Aged Twelve;*

Ghost Town: *Take Two: Royal Pain; Take Two: Black Jack*

Great River Review: *Visit From Donald Justice; Interview, December 1962*

Main Street Rag: *Memo to the Cat Who Keeps Bringing Me
Half-Dead Birds*

Marin Poetry Center Anthologies: *Angel Child/Bathroom Mirror; Back Seat;
Boy Dirty, Aged Twelve*

Marsh Hawk Review: *Alice, Always Alice; Bad Seedling 1929; Garage Note
With Rabbit; Take Two: It's All Greek; Still His House; Ghost Note*

Omniverse: *Sometimes a Horse Is Not a Horse*

PoetryBay: *Momma's Sugar; Clean-Up Man; Memo to the Man Who Gave Me
his Mother's Wedding Ring*

Room of One's Own: *Take Two: Familiar Tense*

River Styx: *Cold Loaves*

Poetry Magazine.com: *Letter to My Daughter* (published as *Death of Boreas*)

Southern Review: *The French Girl Who Would Be Manon; Dish of Mashed Peas*

Talking/Writing: *Letter to My Daughter* (published as *Death of Boreas*)

The Scream Online : *Black Jack / Branwell Bronte and his Drinking Mug*

Tar River: *Acorn Caps as Metaphor; Silverback Dream*

Valley Voices: *Old Beard; Thirst/No Thirst*

Special Thanks to Omnidawn Publishing for permission to publish poems from 2017 pocket book **Take Two: Film Studies.** Also thanks for poems from **Memos,** an Omnidawn pocket book published in 2015.

Special thanks to Conflux Press for poems from **Dreamcrashers,** a chapbook, published in 2016.

Special thanks to Strokestown International Poetry Festival for selectiing "Something Has to Matter" (published as "The Old Bridge, the Woman, and the White Pig") as part of their 20/20 Competion.

Anthologies

Best American Poetry 2015, editors David Lehman & Sherman Alexie: *Memo to the Former Child Prodigy,* Scribner

Changing Harm to Harmony, editor Joseph Zaccardi: *Cross Country; Like It Was,* Marin Poetry Center

Reel Verse: Poems About the Movies, editors Michael Waters & Harold Schechter: *Dashboard Scene / Bonnie Parker and Clyde Barrow,* Knopf—Everyman's Pocket Poets Anthology

Play:

Cutting Ball Theater: *Take Two: Virginia Woolf & Virginia Woolf*

Notes

I
The Girls / The Boys

Each of the *French Girl* and *French Boy* poems in this volume—pages 10, 11, and 18 is based partly on an opera, which is French or one that was originally a French novel or play. In order they are:

Orphée et Eurydice by Christoph Willibald Gluck
Faust by Charles Gounod
Manon Lescaut by Giacomo Puccini

p. 20 A female donkey is called a Jenny.

p. 23 Persephone's other name is *Kore*, meaning "the maiden".

II
Take Two / Film Scenes

This section is a series of filmic scenes about pairs (not always humans) who are headed for disaster, ignominy, or death. Each poem contains [in parentheses] cinematic terms which apply to the current scene. The characters range in time from Medea to Jackie Kennedy and are partly real, partly myth, partly literary. Some of these characters will be more familiar than others—a few less familiar, perhaps:

p. 34 Evelyn Nesbit became notorious when her husband Harry Thaw shot and killed her lover well-known architect Stanford White.

p. 37 George Sand was the pen name of French 19th century novelist named Amatine-Lucile-Aurore Dupin.

p. 49 Assia Wevill was a German born poet whom Ted Hughes lived with when he left Sylvia Plath. Assia, using an oven as Sylvia had, ultimately took her own life as well as the life of the daughter she'd had with Ted.

p. 52 Branwell Bronte was the dissolute brother of the 19th century literary sisters Anne, Emily, & Charlotte Bronte.

III
The Real / The Surreal

p. 62 *Old Beard*: the line *"I can see / my x-rayed heart"* is from Sylvia Plath's poem *Bluebeard*.

p. 67 *Ghost Note*— a ghost note is a musical note with rhythm but no identifiable pitch.

p. 76 *Listen, Young Lover....* — please don't ask about the mouse-skin cape I tried to make for my sister's doll.

p. 85 *Spiritual Carabiner* —Don't ask about the lyra either.

Author Biography

Susan Terris' other recent books are **Take Two: Film Studies** (Omnidawn Publishing), MEMOS (Omnidawn Publishing); and **Ghost of Yesterday** (Marsh Hawk Press). She's published seven books of poetry, 16 chapbooks, three artist's books, and one play. A poem of hers appeared in *Pushcart Prize XXXI*. A poem from **Memos** was in *Best American Poetry 2015*.

Ms. Terris is editor emerita of *Spillway Magazine* and a poetry editor at *Pedestal Magazine*. She lives in San Francisco, except in the summer when she lives by a lake in northern Minnesota.

www.susanterris.com

TITLES FROM MARSH HAWK PRESS

Jane Augustine *Arbor Vitae; KRAZY: Visual Poems and Performance Scripts; Night Lights; A Woman's Guide to Mountain Climbing*

Tom Beckett *Dipstick (Diptych)*

Sigman Byrd *Under the Wanderer's Star*

Patricia Carlin *Original Green; Quantum Jitters; Second Nature*

Claudia Carlson *The Elephant House; My Chocolate Sarcophagus; Pocket Park*

Meredith Cole *Miniatures*

Jon Curley *Hybrid Moments; Scorch Marks*

Neil de la Flor *Almost Dorothy; An Elephant's Memory of Blizzards*

Chard deNiord *Sharp Golden Thorn*

Sharon Dolin *Serious Pink*

Steve Fellner *Blind Date with Cavafy; The Weary World Rejoices*

Thomas Fink *Selected Poems & Poetic Series; Joyride; Peace Conference; Clarity and Other Poems; After Taxes; Gossip: A Book of Poems*

Norman Finkelstein *Inside the Ghost Factory; Passing Over*

Edward Foster *The Beginning of Sorrows; Dire Straits; Mahrem: Things Men Should Do for Men; Sewing the Wind; What He Ought to Know*

Paolo Javier *The Feeling is Actual*

Burt Kimmelman *Abandoned Angel; Somehow*

Burt Kimmelman and Fred Caruso *The Pond at Cape May Point*

Basil King *The Spoken Word / The Painted Hand from Learning to Draw / A History; 77 Beasts: Basil King's Beastiary; Mirage*

Martha King *Imperfect Fit*

Phillip Lopate *At the End of the Day: Selected Poems and An Introductory Essay*

Mary Mackey *Breaking the Fever; The Jaguars That Prowl Our Dreams; Sugar Zone; Travelers With No Ticket Home*

Jason McCall *Dear Hero,*

Sandy McIntosh *A Hole In the Ocean: A Hamptons' Apprenticeship; The After-Death History of My Mother; Between Earth and Sky; Cemetery Chess: Selected and New Poems; Ernesta, in the Style of the Flamenco; Forty-Nine Guaranteed Ways to Escape Death; Obsessional: Poetry for Performance*

Stephen Paul Miller *Any Lie You Tell Will Be the Truth; The Bee Flies in May; Fort Dad; Skinny Eighth Avenue; There's Only One God and You're Not It*

Daniel Morris *Bryce Passage; Hit Play; If Not for the Courage*

Geoffrey O'Brien *The Blue Hill*

Sharon Olinka *The Good City*

Christina Olivares *No Map of the Earth Includes Stars*

Justin Petropoulos *Eminent Domain*

Paul Pines *Charlotte Songs; Divine Madness; Gathering Sparks; Last Call at the Tin Palace*

Jacquelyn Pope *Watermark*

George Quasha *Things Done for Themselves*

Karin Randolph *Either She Was*

Rochelle Ratner *Balancing Acts; Ben Casey Days; House and Home*

Michael Rerick *In Ways Impossible to Fold*

Corrine Robins *Facing It: New and Selected Poems; One Thousand Years; Today's Menu*

Eileen R. Tabios *The Connoisseur of Alleys; I Take Thee, English, for My Beloved; The Light Sang as It Left Your Eyes: Our Autobiography; Reproductions of the Empty Flagpole; Sun Stigmata; The Thorn Rosary: Selected Prose Poems and New (1998–2010)*

Eileen R. Tabios and j/j hastain *The Relational Elations of Orphaned Algebra*

Susan Terris *Ghost of Yesterday; Natural Defenses*

Madeline Tiger *Birds of Sorrow and Joy*

Tana Jean Welch *Latest Volcano*

Harriet Zinnes *Drawing on the Wall; Light Light or the Curvature of the Earth; New and Selected Poems; Weather Is Whether; Whither Nonstopping*

YEAR	AUTHOR	MHP POETRY PRIZE TITLE	JUDGE
2004	Jacquelyn Pope	*Watermark*	Marie Ponsot
2005	Sigman Byrd	*Under the Wanderer's Star*	Gerald Stern
2006	Steve Fellner	*Blind Date With Cavafy*	Denise Duhamel
2007	Karin Randolph	*Either She Was*	David Shapiro
2008	Michael Rerick	*In Ways Impossible to Fold*	Thylias Moss
2009	Neil de la Flor	*Almost Dorothy*	Forrest Gander
2010	Justin Petropoulos	*Eminent Domain*	Anne Waldman
2011	Meredith Cole	*Miniatures*	Alicia Ostriker
2012	Jason McCall	*Dear Hero,*	Cornelius Eady
2013	Tom Beckett	*Dipstick (Diptych)*	Charles Bernstein
2014	Christina Olivares	*No Map of the Earth Includes Stars*	Brenda Hillman
2015	Tana Jean Welch	*Latest Volcano*	Stephanie Strickland
2016	Robert Gibb	*After*	Mark Doty
2017	Geoffrey O'Brien	*The Blue Hill*	Meena Alexander

ARTISTIC ADVISORY BOARD

Toi Derricotte, Denise Duhamel, Marilyn Hacker, Allan Kornblum *(in memorium)*, Maria Mazzioti Gillan, Alicia Ostriker, Marie Ponsot, David Shapiro, Nathaniel Tarn, Anne Waldman, and John Yau.

For more information, please go to: www.marshhawkpress.org